IT TOOK ME 16 MONTHS TO WRITE THIS BOOK. GIVE ME 16 SECONDS TO PERSUADE YOU TO READ IT.

Every human being is endowed with intelligence, memory and strength of character. This role has taught me to touch the hearts of other human beings. I am a happy go lucky daughter of my parents, especially of my mother. My school is proud of me being its student. I am a good friend of my friends who believes in peer learning following my motto, #EachOneTeachTen, which indicates that EACH ONE CAN TEACH ANOTHER TEN PEOPLE, and make global connections. This has an impact that causes a chain reaction that leads to change. I hope my story will inspire you to do the same!

NAMYA JOSHI

#EachOneTeachTen
The Journey Continues...

digcitinstitute **is a community.**

Who We Are

We are community builders who create and facilitate intergenerational learning experiences for communities around the world to be a force for good online at school, home, play, and work.

We are united by the belief that all it takes is one person to stand up and make a difference.

What We Do

Leading by hand, heart, and mind, we transform the narrative around technology and social media through our personalized programs to help guide communities through a process of positive and powerful shifts in how we engage online.

Where to Find Us

You can find our team and community around the world. Our programs and events are available in both English and Spanish.

digcitinstitute
local. global. digital.

What it Looks Like in Action

Our school community approach invites an entire community to learn together. Our programs and events guide administrators, educators, tech integrators, teacher librarians, counselors, athletic departments, parents/caregivers, after school programs, community thought leaders, senior centers, and industry to learn *with* students; creating positive ripples throughout the community.

Learn with Students

Learn with Industry

Learn with Seniors

Our Message to Namya:

Thank you Namya for inspiring your readers to put digital citizenship into action at school, home, play, and work. Your words and actions empower others to want to be a force for good online.

#EachOneTeachTen is not just a motto you live, but a global movement you have created. We invite your readers to get involved by creating more positive ripples in local, global, and digital communities.

digital
citizenship
institute

I am IMPACTOR

I solve real problems in local, global, and digital communities; use tech for good to inspire, and empower others to be the digital

I an INCLUSIVE

I am open to hearing and respectfully recognizing multiple viewpoints and engage with others online with respect and empathy.

I am INFORMED

I evaluate the accuracy, perspective, and validity of digital media and social posts.

I am ENGAGED

I use technology and digital channels for civic engagement, to solve problems and be a force for good in both physical and virtual communities.

I am BALANCED

I make informed decisions about how to prioritize my time and activities online and off.

I am ALERT

I am aware of my online actions, and know how to be safe and create safe spaces for others online.

#EachOneTeachTen – The Journey
Continues

https://xfactoredu.org

X-Factor EDU

Our Mission Statement:

Be Unapologetically You

Table Of Contents

Dedication

For my mother, father, grandparents, school, teachers, educators, and friends who have inspired me throughout my journey and motivated me to never give up and keep on innovating.

Acknowledgment

This book would not have been possible without the help and support of the following people.

My parents Monica Joshi and Kunal Joshi without whom this journey would never have begun. My grandparents, teachers, school, educators, and friends have inspired me to write the book.

Dr. Matthew X. Joseph (X-FactorEdu), has built a platform for taking chances and amplifying the powerful voices of young people like me who have the will to change the world.

Brian Aspinall (Code Breaker Inc), for giving me the wonderful opportunity to publish this book, and whose collaboration and inspiration continue to make a difference in classrooms and schools.

Sarah Laliberte (Editor), for guidance, clarity, support, and for taking the challenge to help make this a better book.

Dr. Marialice B.F.X Curran, Stephen Reid, Pekka Ouli, Bryan Sanders, Ann Kozma, Steve Isaacs, Neha Sehgal, Mrs. Bhupinder Gogia, Meenakshi Uberoi, Garima Babbar, Vinnie Jauhari, and all the educators all over the world for their continued support and words of encouragement.

Community Connect - Humanizing The Effect Of #EachOneTeachTen

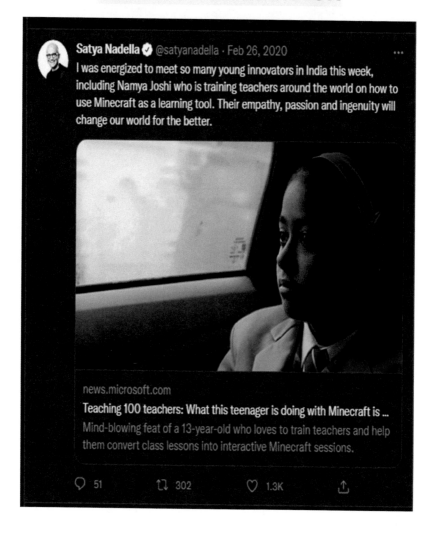

Tweet by Satya Nadella, CEO Microsoft in February 2020 on his visit to India

Tweet by Satya Nadella, CEO Microsoft in
February 2020 on his visit to India

Feedback and tweets from some wonderful students and educators

27 Nov 2019 Satyan Namya Joshi attended a five day exchange program at 'KEOS 2019' in Jyvaskyla, Finland

👤 Online News India 📅 November 27, 2019   A+   A-   🔍

Namya Joshi delivering a keynote at KEOS 2019

Ludhiana, November 27, 2019 (News Team): Namya Joshi, a student of Grade VII of Sat Paul Mittal School and her mentor, Ms. Monica Joshi, IT Head, Sat Paul Mittal School, Global Minecraft Mentor and Microsoft Innovator Educator Expert were invited as the guest speakers at Pavillionjonki, Jyvaskyla, Finland at the event 'KEOS 2019'. They were invited by Poke Vocational College, Äanekoski, Finland. This prestigious program brought together students and educators to showcase their best practices in the digital transformation across the world.

Namya was taken to the tour of different schools. She taught Minecraft at Mikonpuisto Kindergarten School and Telakkakadu Koulu High School. The facilitators as well as the students found it fascinating to use Gamification as an emphatic teaching and learning tool for higher education. She attended a press conference at Mikonpuisto. Unleashing her potential, she also underwent a training cum hands on session on Augmented Reality, 3-D Printing, and Simulators by Poke Vocational College.

Namya delivered a keynote at 'KEOS' and conducted workshops about how literature can be made fun with Minecraft, using interesting ice breaking activities. The presence of Ministers, Directors, and Principals of Finnish Schools made the event even more significant. Ms. Monica Joshi also conducted workshops wherein she taught Minecraft, Wakelet, Flipgrid and other MS Tools.

Namya was also invited at Edu Days event organized by Microsoft at Gurugram. She had the proud privilege to share the stage with Mr. Anant Maheshwari, President Microsoft, India wherein she left everyone spell bound with her nimble wit and subject expertise. He applauded her for training not only her peers but also teachers across India, Vietnam, Hungary and Finland, thus empowering them to use Minecraft, Flipgrid, Kahoot and Forms in the classrooms.

Ms. Bhupinder Gogia, Principal, Sat Paul Mittal School, congratulated Namya Joshi on her remarkable accomplishment and wished her luck for the future endeavours. She was ecstatic, acknowledging the efforts put in by the mentors at Sat Paul Mittal School to fulfil the vision of the school to nurture empowered leaders of tomorrow leading to a consistently high level of pupil achievement.

Press coverage of my Finland visit as a Keynote speaker at KEOS2019

Prologue

"To get through the hardest journey, we need to take only one step at a time, but we must keep on stepping"
Chinese Proverb

I'd like to show my gratitude to everyone who has contributed to my continuous journey. First and foremost, I'd like to express my gratitude to Mr. Narendra Modi, Prime Minister of India, whose vision of a self-reliant India has always inspired me to keep doing what I'm doing. I'd like to express my gratitude to my parents and grandparents, who have always been supportive of me and have given me great principles such as never giving up and never stopping innovating. My school, including the principal, teachers, and friends, have always been incredibly supportive of everything I do and have always praised me for my accomplishments. Also, I want to thank all of the educators from around the world with whom I had the pleasure of collaborating and from whom I learned a great deal. Let's embark on a fascinating voyage that you, my readers, will surely love.

Foreword

By Stephen Reid
@StephenReidEdu
Game-Base Learning Lead at Microsoft

Mentor
verb

To help and give advice to a younger or
less experienced person, especially in a job or at school.

The Cambridge Dictionary defines the word mentor as above. The
exchange of help and advice from the older and more experienced
to the younger and less experienced. And so it is that we assume
and have always assumed that it should be. That the natural order
of knowledge transfer must be from the old to the young, and the
former must automatically have the advantage of experience.

As an educator, I've always struggled with this definition of the
word mentor. Never assuming that I am ever the expert in any
given room and in particular, the classroom. Yet, our entire
education system worldwide has been based, and largely remains
based, on the assumption of age and experience as a framework for
success. A system in which teachers teach and students get taught.

So let's now consider the Cambridge Dictionary definition of an

Expert:

Expert
noun

A person with a high level of knowledge or skill relating to a particular subject or activity.

Note that there is no reference to age or status. Simply the recognition of knowledge or skill in a given field. Almost at odds with the definition of a Mentor.

The world is changing faster than even the most engaged technologists and largest technology organizations can keep up with, and with it a new age of technology in education is dawning. An age that will transform our curricula, pedagogical practices, and assessment models worldwide, whether we are ready or not. An age in which students will adopt and deploy technology for learning themselves, seeking relevance and meaning in their learning and preparing for a life beyond school through digital means. With the development and introduction of AI, VR, Game-Based Learning, Big Data, and Cloud Computing, as well as a global emphasis on greater diversity and inclusion than ever, students are leading their own learning and taking us with them in their wake.

In 2015 I ran a project in partnership with the BBC in which I created a scale map of Scotland in Minecraft and asked over 10,000 students to use the map to create their 'Built Environment'. A study of their local area and its 'most important features and landmarks. At the time, the program's sponsors planned to take these builds and use them to display Scotland's urban and suburban heritage. It was assumed that the results likely included our famous castles, ancient landmarks, most prestigious homes. The results, however, were quite different. Students instead built their local skate park, police station, supermarket, mall, and cinema. They focussed on details such as branded stores, movie posters, and pathways through parks linking one place to another. They even added recycling centers. They created maps of cities and towns, the likes of which the sponsors had never imagined nor could understand. The program served to highlight how utterly blind the adults in charge were to the worldview of our children. What is important to them? Where do they go, what do they do, who and what do they value, how do they view their environment, and perhaps most importantly, why?

I myself wasn't surprised. I have long believed that we must all be mindful of the need to surround ourselves with a rich and diverse range of mentors. Younger as well as older. Hearts and minds that experience the world in ways we ourselves cannot. Seeing, hearing and feeling what we do not. And so I spent most of my time seeking out these mentors. Listening, learning, and being led by their thoughts, opinions and ideas. I happily credit much of my early success in technology in education to my younger mentors, less so to my own peers and certainly my own teachers.

It is in practicing this that I discovered the wonder of Namya Joshi. A young woman who holds her expertise above her age and status yet remains humble and curious. A young female forging territory in still largely male-dominated spaces. A young student who is building her experience in landscapes, most adults are still afraid to tread. Namya is unafraid to try. To fail. To learn. To grow. She explores and takes risks. She reaches out to those she needs to learn from. Audits and assesses the tools presented to her before applying them to her world. And in doing so, she is a Mentor to those very same adults. Boldly challenging education and all that we believe is the order of things. Her vision of 'Each One Teach Ten' through mentorship is one the education system and all in it can learn from. Namya follows her heart, interests, and instinct for what the world asks of her. She poses a gentle yet determined challenge to a world obsessed with uniform curriculum, uniform delivery, and uniform assessment.

Namya is my mentor, and I would urge anyone reading this to not only embrace her alike but to look around at the younger mentors in your life; for a while, they may not have the age and experience determined to be important enough to teach, they are without doubt the pioneers of tomorrow's world and tomorrow's classroom.

Introduction

Do you know that only about a quarter of STEM workers, i.e. 28%, are women? When I talk about STEM workers, I mean engineers, scientists, architects, mathematicians, etc. The mindset of society seems to be that only males can dominate in such fields. We are living in the 21st century where we talk about equipping all children with the 6 C's (Communication, Collaboration, Creativity, Critical Thinking, Citizenship, and Character). Then Why, WHY in this day and age have we not been able to achieve gender balance and gender equality?

I am Namya Joshi, a proud Indian girl. I have spent the last four years designing and delivering free-of-cost coding workshops for more than 15,000 teachers and young people, especially girls, in India and all over the world. I have also been empowering other young people to run their own coding clubs. I have raised awareness about social issues using game-based learning with STEM.

It all started four years ago during an unplanned interaction with my teacher. I had been glued to a game called Minecraft. We all know that Minecraft is used for gaming but soon I realised that it can be used for serious education also. I suggested this to my teacher and I created my first lesson on Egyptian civilization. The lesson was a great success! Both the teacher and students were happy with the outcomes. The teacher observed that students were more engaged with self-paced learning since they could revisit concepts they didn't understand and perform their evaluations in a non-threatening environment. This experience empowered me, and I moved on to training more peers and teachers.

I am inspired by my own motto, #EachOneTeachTen, which means EACH ONE PERSON can TEACH another TEN people. Then those ten can share the knowledge with another ten, and so on... In this way, the impact of teaching each person is multiplied. The biggest weapon for change is knowledge, so I will continue to share my knowledge with other teachers and students. I follow the motto of #EachOneTeachTen so that my unique knowledge will create the ripples of change needed to achieve the United Nations Sustainable Development Goals for 2030. I hope my story will inspire you to do the same!

My Personality
Chapter 1

"Personality is the awareness of our uniqueness in relation to the rest of the universe."
Ernest Dimnet

H-Y-P-E-R-A-C-T-I-V-E. Get that? Well, I have always been a hyperactive child since birth, i.e. 21st November 2006, 3:00 a.m. Nah! Just kidding. But it's very true that I was born exactly at 3:00 a.m. To be honest, I have no recollection of how I was between the ages of 0 and 4, which is understandable. Now, talking about being hyperactive—don't take it negatively. I was hyperactive to learn, to try new things, and to break things. Okay, I guess I am being very goofy, so let's put this to rest and return to the primary matter.

Anyways, I proudly take this opportunity to introduce my real self to you. In school and at home, I've always been an inquisitive child. I just love asking questions. Though I ask questions at school to clarify my uncertainties or if something else comes to mind, occasionally I get the impression that the teacher thinks I am testing her expertise. Well, that's not true. Questions and I can't seem to keep away from each other. In reality, asking questions is beneficial since it reassures you that your brain is functioning properly. It is a proven fact that half of your brain does not operate properly if you are not curious. Inquisitiveness keeps your intellect active rather than inactive. Curious people always ask questions and search for answers.

I have always adored the word creative because I like to be creative in every way possible. Once my teacher asked me which skill of mine I am proud of. Unquestionably my answer was creativity. I'm not praising myself, I'm simply being honest. We all know the fact that humans can't fit into small boxes, but their brains can. Well, some minds are too big to fit into any box! Why do you think that is? Because... they think outside the box. Everyone learns uniquely, but these individuals think uniquely. Yes, that is also one of my characteristics. I believe such traits are inherited from my mother since I have always observed her thinking from a unique standpoint. I consider myself extremely fortunate to have gained such virtues from her. Thinking beyond the box has helped me gain a wider perspective, produce high-quality work, solve problems more creatively, differentiate myself from others, think critically, and remain adaptive in any environment.

My next outstanding characteristic is my ability to work in a group. I'm always delighted to work with my teammates whenever we are divided into teams. That delight, I believe, is what enabled me to cooperate with others and improve my communication abilities. When I was in elementary school and working on projects in groups, a few classmates always tried to disappoint me by disagreeing with my ideas, even if they were good. For a few hours or perhaps days, I was affected by their actions towards me. Later on, I realised that they were attempting to divert my focus from my main goal, so I stopped paying attention to them. This experience taught me how to deal with difficult circumstances and convince people to listen to my point of view. I didn't want to be subdued by them, so I learned to fight back for the greater good. Fighting is not referred to as martial arts in this context, but rather as communicating my views to others in such a way that they eventually agree with me. It's interesting and ironic that those who have never recognized any of my ideas as true suddenly say, "Let's ask Namya, she knows more and might be able to help us."

I realized that life is more than my school's four walls and the hundred students that reside within them; it is also about the outside world. My hidden talent has always been writing and sharing my thoughts. I used to keep journals and write blog posts to make sense of what I was going through. Before I'd feel all of the tensions of the day, large and small, piling up within my brain, or I'd just shut myself and refuse to speak to anyone. It wasn't until I got into the practice of reading and writing for myself that I began to see a decrease in the intensity of the emotion. It's crucial to have a way to express your thoughts and sentiments, and it can be something other than artistic. Going on a stroll, putting on headphones and listening to new music, exercising, or reading can all help.

In my whole life (15 years), I have never been an introvert. I enjoy making connections with others and conversing with them. I'm not an extrovert either; I'm just a regular person. I don't think being an introvert is an issue as long as you're being yourself and not trying to be someone else, and silence is indeed a source of tremendous strength. But don't forget to say what you're thinking because of #EveryVoiceMatters. Apart from the qualities I mentioned, I am a cheerful person who enjoys eating. In the next chapters, you'll learn more about my current self. What are you waiting for? Go ahead and flip the page!!

Quote By - Jan Phillips
Art By - Namya Joshi

Love For Technology
Chapter 2

Innovation is fueled by technology. Technology is fueling innovation. The ability of people to compete in the twenty-first century will be determined by their use of technology
Namya Joshi.

This is why I adore technology: it can provide you with both power and privacy if utilized correctly.

I would like to share some fascinating knowledge about DNA with you before I start spilling the beans about my love for technology. Deoxyribonucleic acid, or DNA, is the molecule that holds an organism's genetic code. Animals, plants, protists, archaea, and bacteria are all included. Each cell in the organism has DNA, which instructs the cells on how to produce proteins. Most importantly, DNA is inherited by children from their parents. Both of my parents work in the IT sector, so I guess I have DNA to thank for my interest in IT!. I grew up witnessing my parents utilise IT tools, and it sparked my curiosity. So, anytime they took a break from using their gadgets, I looked at some of those applications, and guess what? I accidentally erased my mother's important file one time. Luckily I was able to restore it by magic (Ctrl + Z, LOL). I am very good at cracking PJs. PJ = Poor, Pathetic, or Perfect Jokes and I've got all three kinds of jokes in store. For the same reason, my friends refer to me as a PJ girl.

I've enjoyed competing since I was a kid because it allows us to learn to deal with opposing viewpoints and ideas, interact with people who have very different personalities, and manage subjectivity in everyday life. Speaking, debating, and technology are the competitions I always look forward to. Speaking because I enjoy sharing my opinions with others, debating because it allows me to express myself, and technology because it is my strongest suit. I began my technology journey by learning MS Paint, MS

Word, MS PowerPoint, Tux Paint, and Movie Maker, then progressed to a variety of tools that I use today. From the day I discovered WhizJuniors, my enthusiasm for technology grew even more. To tell you the truth, my entire epic journey of using Minecraft to help individuals began through WhizJuniors. I learned a lot of things like Canva, Google Suite, MS Office tools, Prezi, Scratch, WordPress, etc. Winning coins for finishing each task, posting certifications, and receiving positive feedback always encouraged me to pursue more courses. I finished all the courses in just over a year! I loved taking these courses since there was something new to learn every day. The nicest part was reading the kind comments on the certifications I submitted since it lifted my confidence and showed me what new things I could achieve.

Now, these online courses were also a competition in which participants competed against one another, with those who placed in the top 20 nationwide qualifying for the finals in Mumbai. I secured second place and qualified for the finals. When I got the results, I was on cloud nine. That was my second trip to Mumbai, popularly known as the "Land of Seven Islands." I couldn't wait to meet the other finalists and learn more about them. When we arrived, we were greeted by the organisers and given instructions on how to proceed to the final round. It was a 20-question quiz and the one who completed it the quickest and with the most accuracy won. I was nervous at first, but witnessing everyone else's nervousness helped me feel less alone. After the round, it was time for the results. I was hoping to win, but it wasn't my day that day. I stood there cheering for the three winners, promising myself that if I worked harder, I'd be there in first place next year, accepting the award.

The goal here wasn't so much to win the award as it was to learn how to work hard for everything you want. It does not come without difficulty. It takes a lot of time and work. That's what I did. I worked extra hard to improve the quality of my certifications and to prepare for the quizzes. What's more, the following year, I was named the TOP TECH SAVVY STUDENT in INDIA. This accomplishment marked the start of my path toward my life's objective. I received a trophy, a laptop, and a certificate as a prize. At that point, I discovered I was the only female among the winners; the others were all boys. Although I believe in gender equality and that everyone should be treated equally, it seemed to me at the time that there must be a dearth of knowledge for so many girls to be unaware of such opportunities. That's what motivated me to start encouraging girls to pursue careers in STEM disciplines. If you're interested in learning how, keep reading.

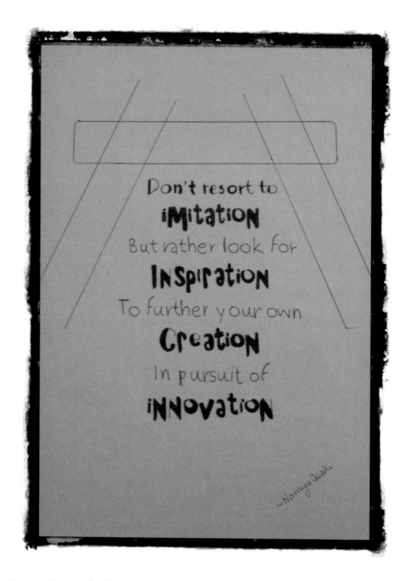

Don't resort to
iMitatioN
But rather look for
INspiratioN
To further your own
CreatioN
In pursuit of
iNNovatioN

~Namya Joshi

Quote By - Ashwini N C
Art By - Namya Joshi

Hunger To Learn
Chapter 3

"No one can assist you if you are unwilling to learn. No one can stop you if you are determined to learn."
Zig Ziglar

From the beginning of time, learning has been the backbone of mankind's existence. Man needs to learn and find new ways of doing things and enjoying life, whether through official or informal schooling. We learn directly or indirectly from the moment we are born until we die. Humans have grown with a hunger for learning as a part of their everyday lives as a result of being born into a new world, observing their parents and those around them, going to school, interacting with peers, experiencing the workplace, and eventually having to learn about the changing generation from their grandchildren. And my desire to learn is insatiable. Every day, I pick up some new information.

Apart from sports and computer applications, I continue to be quite interested and involved in extracurricular activities as a child. I take part in such events not only for the chance to win, but also to acquire a new talent that I've never attempted before. During the Diwali (an Indian festival) celebrations in my school when I was in the fifth grade, a competition for card-making was held. I was looking forward to it because I enjoy making cards. Unfortunately, my card was disqualified as I had used a colored sheet to make it. Because it was only a competition, I didn't feel discouraged. We then proceeded outdoors to create a Rangoli (designs made with powdered colours on the floor).

I did feel that my card was pretty beautiful. The same day, I came to know about an online exam called Intellithon. There were a lot of competitions in which we could participate and there were several prizes. So I applied for the Diwali card-making contest and submitted the same card as my entry for that. The results were supposed to be out in a week or so. I received the results a few days later, in the evening, and guess what? I came in first. I was awarded a cash prize of 5000 INR. I understood that being acknowledged only inside the confines of your school isn't what life is all about. Outside of your school, there is a whole other universe that will help you achieve anything in life while also teaching you how to live in the real world and interact with all types of people. And it was at this point that I began to engage in competitions outside of school more frequently, which provided me with a lot of exposure and fueled my desire to learn and do new things. (I'm just mentioning this historical knowledge in case someone reads this book in 100 years!)

Quote By- Kurt Cobain
Art By- Namya Joshi

#EachOneTeachTen

A Whole New World Of Minecraft
Chapter 4

You just know when it's time to start something new, and you have faith in the magic of fresh beginnings.
Namya Joshi

Welcome to the main chapter of this book, which might be the main reason you decided to read the book in the first place. MINECRAFT. So let's start from the beginning. This term was first introduced to me in fourth grade. How? So, I was playing a word search on my mother's laptop when I accidentally clicked on the start icon, and the first word that came up was "Minecraft." I switched from the word search game to Minecraft. All I saw when the window opened was a black screen with greenish-grey letters spelling out the name Minecraft. Okay, so you're probably going to think I'm crazy if I tell you this, but I am not sure how I came up with such an idea. I mistook the name MINECRAFT for MINE, which implies my, and CRAFT, which is similar to papercraft. I am not even joking. My mother soon arrived, and I asked if I might play, but she simply stated that it doesn't work. I stood up and walked into my room to study after staring at the computer for a bit.

Three months went by, and I was going to be promoted to the fifth grade in a few months. Minecraft was never a thought that came to mind for me. Then one day, while working on a project on my laptop, I accidentally clicked on the start icon again, and guess what appeared? It was, of course, my beloved Minecraft! So I simply clicked on it to test whether it now works. I waited a few seconds for the screen to appear, but this time it wasn't like the others. I could see Play, Setting, and Marketplace symbols. I was so delighted that I opened it and it worked. Well, I believe my laptop was fortunate. I didn't waste any time and began playing right away. My mother came into my room after about fifteen minutes and spotted me playing. She inquired as to what I was up to. I told her I was playing Minecraft. She was taken aback when I told her I knew how to play it. So I spent approximately two months playing Minecraft.

Then when I was in fifth grade, I realised that learning through text-based books was not simple for everyone. I observed that several of my friends were having difficulty grasping some of the more difficult topics. I was able to grasp them since I paid attention in class, but what about others who may have difficulties while learning or who, despite attentive listening, are unable to comprehend it? I assumed that someone would take action, but it didn't take me long to realise that, that someone was myself.

It was simply another day when I received a notification on my laptop about something connected to Minecraft Education Edition while working on a project. I had no idea that Minecraft had many editions at the time. So, as I finished my project, I decided to open it and have a look at it. The Education Edition asked me to check in using a Microsoft ID when I first launched it. I had won a poetry recitation competition earlier that day, so I asked my mum to obtain me an ID and password for it. Fortunately, she consented and gave it to me. I began to delve more into it and became completely immersed in the beautiful world of learning through Minecraft.

One day at my school, a Minecraft workshop for teachers was held. We students were required to instruct them on how to use Minecraft. At that very moment, the notion occurred to me: "Why don't we use Minecraft in education?" Yes, I considered moving away from merely gaming and towards instructional gaming, or 'Gamification In Education.' My mother, a Minecraft Mentor, had been introduced to Minecraft being utilised in many aspects a few months earlier, so I went to her and informed her about my plans to develop educational courses for the classroom in Minecraft Education. She was surprised by my concept and agreed to help me out.

However, when I presented these ideas to my teachers, they were sceptical. They had never seen gaming employed in education before, especially when the general public believes that games are a waste of time or that they cause us to become hyperactive or something similar. I had things planned at the time, such as working hard to alter people's attitudes about games, as well as changing the way we learn, and moving the classroom atmosphere toward practical, gamified, and STEM learning. In the early months of sixth grade, I produced my first Egyptian civilization lesson in Minecraft Education Edition and showed it to my history instructor. She was the first instructor to accept my lesson and agreed to use it in class to help students understand the subject. And, guess what, it was a huge hit! I could notice the difference right away; the kids were more interested since they found visual and game-based learning to be a more effective means of understanding the courses, which led to increased student engagement in the classrooms.

The outcomes pleased both the teacher and the pupils. Students were more engaged in self-paced learning because they could revisit subjects they didn't grasp and complete their assessments in a non-threatening atmosphere. As I observed the improvements in the classroom, I began to develop more lessons for various areas. Then I took it a step further and began teaching kids and teachers at my school and in my city how to utilise Minecraft and other gamified technologies that I was learning at the time. When I was in sixth grade, I ran an Introduction to Minecraft workshop at my school for 200 students in grades 4 and 5, and the kids handed me gratitude cards because they thoroughly enjoyed the session, giving me even more incentive to keep doing what I'm doing.

Quote By- Unknown
Drawing By- Namya Joshi

Taking It Forward
Chapter 5

We continue to go forward, opening new doors and doing new things because we are interested, and curiosity leads us down new routes.
Namya Joshi

When I taught individuals about Minecraft and got them involved in various activities, I was able to develop certain aspects of their character and personality. Some important vocational skills they learned were leadership, collaboration, and ICT (Information and Communications Technology) readiness. Leadership was the first skill to be learned. Leadership is a critical skill because good leaders enable an organisation to increase efficiency and reach their goals. Effective leaders clarify an organisation's objective and encourage employees. Collaboration is the second skill, and it improves productivity and provides employees with a feeling of purpose in the business. It's also simpler to come up with new ideas to solve an issue or to complete the task on time. Then there are ICT skills, which are required for the majority of professions. These abilities will aid you in organising your workload, streamlining procedures, and gaining access to digital information. Improving your ICT abilities is a reasonable approach to offer yourself a competitive advantage over other applicants when looking for employment.

Some other important skills that were learned were empathy, creativity, communication, and general knowledge. Empathy is something that I am very passionate about. It is a critical skill because it allows us to understand how others feel so we can respond correctly. It's usually linked to social behaviour, and there's a lot of evidence that having more empathy leads to more helpful behaviour. Then there's creativity, which enables us to approach and solve issues more openly and innovatively. The mind is opened through creativity. A culture that has lost touch with its creative side is imprisoned, and generations of people may be closed-minded as a result. It broadens our horizons and might assist us in overcoming prejudices. We can adjust to the physical and social aspects of work with the aid of communication. It also enhances the industry's human relations. An effective communication system allows management to encourage, influence, and gratify subordinates, which increases morale and keeps employees engaged. Lastly, people gained general knowledge, which improves our thinking and problem-solving abilities. Brains work more easily and effectively when they have a firm foundation of information. With the power of information, we grow smarter and more capable of solving difficulties.

So, one day, I was simply having fun watching television when my mother walked into my room and informed me that I had a Skype session with instructors and that I needed to lead a beginners Minecraft session for them. Yes, that is precisely how my mother said it. She has a propensity for surprising me with information. I was completely baffled. "Namya, you can do it," I told myself, and then I went ahead and led the session. I was worried at first, but because I was familiar with Minecraft, I eventually gained confidence while teaching them. After the session, the teachers complimented me on how effectively I taught, which encouraged me to believe that I might be a good instructor for others.

Another thing I learned was that it can be difficult to answer a lot of questions without frowning. The teachers asked me many questions throughout the session, and sometimes I wondered why they couldn't grasp concepts that felt basic to me. But this improved my ability to empathise with others. Later on, I began to broaden my horizons by educating instructors and kids around my state and nation. Every time I led a class, I had an amazing chance to learn something new. Aside from that, I enrolled in several programs to acquire new technologies that I was unfamiliar with so I could try to apply them to game-based learning for classroom engagement.

While designing Minecraft, I became more interested in STEM and STEAM. I discovered that there are extremely few girls involved in these disciplines. So every time I won a tournament, I would always ask my school principal to give me a chance to speak at the podium. I always said, "I wish there were more women in this industry. So, girls, let's get ready!" Later on, I started a GirlsInSTEM club wherein I taught girls about different tools and I learned from them too. Then I built the most well-known universe, The Magical World Of Books, inside Minecraft. This world benefits SDG (Sustainable Development Goals) 2030, focusing on SDG Goal No. 4 (Quality Education). The Magical World of Books portrays visual learning and educational equity for all. I have made worlds like Harry Potter, Epic Ramayana, Mickey Mouse Clubhouse, Dr. A.P.J. Abdul Kalam Biographies, Piispala Youth Summer Camp, and many others. I won the UNESCO Worldwide Clubs Multimedia Competition for this. So that's how it proceeded from there; the more I made and shared, the more people appreciated me.

Quote By- Zig Ziglar
Art By- Namya Joshi

Going Global Physically
Chapter 6

Experiences should be a part of your life. It's not about possessions. Have tales to convey rather than things to display.
Namya Joshi

After I began working more in Minecraft, I was given an opportunity to collaborate with Mr. Pekka Ouli in Finland on a Christmas project to make a Minecraft jingle, for which I was well appreciated. Then, in November 2019, I was given an unimaginable opportunity: I was invited to Finland to present a workshop for university professors and professionals. Being invited to another nation and conducting training as a keynote speaker was like a dream come true. I went there with my mother on 11th November. We flew from Delhi to Doha, which is in Qatar, and we arrived there at 3:00 p.m. Our flight to Helsinki was scheduled for 1:00 a.m. the next day. We hadn't intended to go out and explore the area because it was our first trip without my father and we were terrified of getting lost or stuck in traffic. Now, comes the question of what would we do for these 9 HOURS at the airport? So, here's the solution. First, we had a thorough tour of the airport, which was truly quite lovely. It has many shopping malls, which we visited one by one, taking our time in each one. Exploring the entire mall and burning several calories while walking made us hungry. As a result, we decided to stop at an airport restaurant for a nice meal. We placed an order for pizza, pastries, and cola and decided to watch some YouTube videos after we finished our meal. What's more, I watched three Harry Potter movies in one sitting, which caused the phone to plead for a recharge. So I put the phone on charge and decided to read some books.

Now comes the moment when we have two hours until our flight. We were literally dozing off. Finally, we boarded the plane, and as soon as I sat down in my seat, I fell asleep (I had no idea we were already flying XD). We reached Finland in the early morning. It's a stunningly gorgeous location known as the Land of Lakes, with 188,000 lakes to be exact. It's fantastic! Two amusing things happened to us as soon as we arrived. First, when we arrived at the metro station to travel to Helsinki, the ticket machine only accepted a particular coin. So we had to run back to the airport to the money transfer centre and then back to the metro station. Then, when we arrived at our Helsinki metro station, we heard an announcement saying that the platform number had changed and that the train will arrive in the next five minutes, but we had no idea what it meant. Thankfully, two helpful individuals were standing nearby who explained that we needed to quickly go to another platform. We thanked them and dashed towards the subway, to get to the train.

The journey from Helsinki to Jyvaskyla took three and a half hours. I slept the entire trip since I was fatigued. Then when we arrived in Jyvaskyla, we met Mr. Pekka Ouli who was waiting for us and drove us to Äänekoski, my favourite city in Finland. We arrived at the hotel, unloaded our belongings, ate dinner, and went to our rooms. We slept with our sweaters on at night, assuming it would be cold. However, we were surprised to find ourselves sweating. That's when we noticed the rooms were centrally heated. Also, it was always dark by 4:00 p.m. every day which was very amusing.

On the first day, we walked down to have breakfast and met Ms. Sara Abou, a Lebanon-based Minecraft mentor. Mr. Pekka then drove us to Mikonpuisto Kindergarten, where I worked on a Christmas project with him virtually. There, I taught Minecraft to children aged 3 to 5 years old using Minecraft Java Edition, which was my first time using that version. Then we proceeded to the POKE Vocational College, where we observed students over the age of 18 studying various skills, such as how to create paper in the Chemistry lab and making little vehicles with Raspberry Pi in the Lego Lab. I learned how to use virtual reality headsets and observed how 3D models are created. I was also given one as a present. So the day progressed with a lot of VR exploration.

The next day, we visited a Finnish school where we met the principal and were given a tour of the facility. Afterward, we went to the POKE simulator lab to learn how to use a virtual reality game to operate a tree cutter. Guess what? After learning how to play the game, I was able to drive a large machine on my own, despite not having a driver's licence. That was a once-in-a-lifetime experience. We also shot the KEOS 2019 event's introductory video. The most memorable was the cultural dinner at Mr. Pekka's residence later that evening. We all prepared our favourite foods. I also met Sanni, one of his daughters. Playing video games with her was one of the most splendid things to do. She is also a great pianist.

The following day was spent preparing for our presentations. We also went to the Jyväskylä Paviljonki to put up our presentation materials and have a look around. I was very enthusiastic about my presentation and put in a lot of preparation time. The big day had arrived: Saturday, November 16, 2019. At the age of eleven, I gave my first keynote workshop, where I discussed Minecraft and game-based learning in schools in front of educators and professionals from several colleges, including Finland's education minister. At noon I had another lecture on the same topic, but this time with different professors. It was a wonderful opportunity. Isn't it true that all of this called for a celebration? We had a great time at a restaurant named Harald. This encounter was simply too wonderful to put into words. But there were two things that I liked best: one, my mother was proud of me, and second, Mr. Pekka stated he would sell my presentation for $100 million if he could. I will be eternally thankful to Mr. Pekka for this wonderful opportunity, which provided me with many new perspectives on the outside world.

Quote By- Pema Chodron
Art By- Namya Joshi

Surprise Landing
Chapter 7

Life is so amazing. Surprising delights await you around the most unexpected corners.
Namya Joshi

This isn't the conclusion of the tale. We left Äänekoski for Helsinki to catch a flight to India the next day. When we arrived in Helsinki, we needed to locate the hotel where we would stay. It was close to the bus station. We stepped out of the bus terminal with our hefty luggage. First and foremost, we had no idea where to go. My father had sent my mother a link to a Google map, but there was no internet. So he gave us the offline map, but it didn't recognize our steps. That scenario was quite irritating. But, thanks to the assistance of a friendly lady, we were able to locate our accommodations. When we went to buy breakfast in the morning, we learned that it was just a few steps away from the bus terminal but we couldn't see it.

While in Finland, I was informed that Mr. Anant Maheshwary, President of Microsoft India, wished to see me the day we landed in Delhi, India for EduDays 2019. I was ecstatic to meet such a prominent figure. I assumed that I would meet him in his office and that he would ask me a few questions. It didn't quite come out the way I had hoped. I arrived in Delhi at 7:00 or 8:00 a.m. We sat in the cab on our way to the EduDays event location. I hurriedly changed into my school clothes as soon as I arrived. THEN THE MOST SURPRISING MOMENT HAPPENED. When I arrived, the organisers informed me that he wanted to meet me on stage in front of educators from all across India. I was taken aback. I was shivering. At the moment, I was experiencing a roller coaster of emotions. But I overcame my anxiety and entered the place. They instructed me to take a seat next to Mr. Anant. He has a pleasant demeanour, as seen by the fact that he initiated a discussion with me, which helped to calm me down. Then he walked on stage and introduced me to all of the educators, inviting me to take the platform. He asked me three questions in all. I was able to respond to his questions.

I may appear to be self-assured on the surface, but I was quite scared on the inside. When I told Mr. Anant that I wanted to work at Microsoft, he was ecstatic and burst out laughing. My YouTube channel, TechnocratNJ, has the video available. As soon as my meeting with Mr. Anant ended, educators began praising me, asking me several questions, and asking me to sit with them and share my journey till now. We arrived at our hotel in the evening, and I was unexpectedly energised. My mother gave me pills to avoid jet lag after I freshened up. To be honest, I didn't even have the stamina to eat dinner and I was fast asleep after five minutes. However, after my mother woke me and persuaded me, I went to the dining hall for dinner. I talked to my grandparents at the end of the day. The day went well. To be honest, I had never experienced anything like this before. I had the impression that they thought I was a celebrity. It was a beautiful event that gave me confidence in my chosen route.

Quote By- Pema Chodron
Art By- Namya Joshi

Young Innovators Summit
Chapter 8

*Inspiration responds to our attention in a variety of ways,
some of which are unexpected.*
Namya Joshi

I went on vacation with my family to Himachal Pradesh in January 2021. During the holidays, I received a call from the Microsoft office announcing the Young Innovator's Summit, which would take place in February. The fact that Mr. Satya Nadella, CEO of Microsoft, would be meeting us was the biggest surprise. That made me extremely happy. Before the final presentation, we had some online rehearsals with the organisers. I found out that two more people had been invited. One of them was Prateek Mohapatra, the global champion of the Imagine Cup in the big data category, and is currently a Microsoft Product Manager. The other was Ishlok Vashistha, Co-Founder of Caeli. He had created a mask that is also a personal air filter that you can wear on your face. It's the most advanced air mask on the market, filtering out pollutants and germs while allowing for easy breathing. With the Caeli Evo, you get the best of both worlds: all-day comfort and head-turning style. I was completely enthralled by what they had created. They appreciated me greatly and were astounded to see how I created study materials utilising a game application, Minecraft. It was a great feeling for me to connect with them.

So, I arrived in Delhi a day before I met the organisers so that we could all practise speaking on stage while answering some of the questions posed by the moderator, Mr. Bhaskar Basu. After the rehearsal, Prateek told me that Mr. Nadella had referenced me at his Bengaluru summit and had shown a video about my Minecraft journey there. It was a tremendous honour for me. This just increased my anticipation for the next day's event. We arrived at the venue about 9:00 a.m. the next day since we needed to do a run-through before the event. I was brimming with excitement since we were going to meet him before presenting on stage. We entered the room, and I noticed a few students giving him presentations on their projects. We soon had the opportunity to meet him and take photographs with him. "How did you come up with the idea of using a game like Minecraft for game-based learning?" he inquired. I gladly responded by informing him about my journey.

We then took the stage and gave a presentation, answering a few questions about our journey and work. It was a wonderful day for me, filled with unexpected events such as reporters seeing me and repeatedly calling me for interviews, as well as opportunities to learn new things. He also posted a tweet on Twitter about me, which made me giddy with delight and gratitude. This event was indeed a turning point in my journey because it motivated me to take my venture forward.

Quote By- Unknown
Art By- Namya Joshi

No Lockdown For Learning
Chapter 9

Live as if you were to die tomorrow. Learn as if you were to live forever."
Mahatma Gandhi

The year 2020 will go down in history as one of the most memorable. As my involvement with STEM grew, more like-minded people began to join me in my journey, enhancing my life. But the Covid-19 pandemic resulted in a significant loss of human life around the world and posed an unprecedented threat to public health, food systems, and the workplace. The pandemic wreaked havoc on the economy and society, putting tens of millions of people at risk of sinking into abject poverty. But during these tough times, there was No Lockdown For Learning.

When we heard about the tremendous deaths and devastation, we were all terrified. The entire planet was placed on lockdown, and India went into lockdown on March 22, 2020. For the first few days, we all liked the calming rhythm of having no routine.
I'm sure we've all had our share of difficulties. The choice is yours whether you run the day or the day runs you. I was determined to stick to my routine as I walked to school. My private life did not come to a close. To have a happy life, we must confront and change our irregular lives into regular ones, which I do by staying occupied. I devised a timetable that I faithfully followed and truly enjoyed. I drew the timetables out on paper and embellished the drawings to make them more interesting and not monotonous.

My day started at 5.30 a.m. with Sehaj Yog (meditation for balancing the seven chakras inside the body) and exercise, as producing happy hormones is crucial. I made the most of my time in the midst of these trying times. This was the time when I learned to programme, develop graphics, create websites, and play the piano. It was critical to go through these principles again. On Twitter and LinkedIn, I started teaching free classes for these applications. I couldn't believe I was able to train over 1000 teachers and students in just four months, and that I was able to post lessons for students and teachers every day. My editing and presentation skills improved as a result of this.

I felt compelled deep down inside to start my own club exclusively for girls. The skills I learned during the lockdown gave me strength, and they helped me launch the #GirlsInStem group. I was pleased when my friends and kids, as well as educators, from other schools tagged me on Twitter and LinkedIn after successfully completing a task or obtaining an award. This was the epitome of my #EachOneTeachTen credo. Defying all odds during the pandemic and collaborating with 98 countries to promote education during the troubled times of Coronavirus-induced lockdown, I created a virtual library of over 200 lessons that are available free of charge on my YouTube channel (TechnocratNJ) and on my website (www.namyajoshi.com). I led over 100 seminars and assisted instructors in developing remote learning tutorials. I gave more than 100 talks on various platforms to close the gender gap in STEM, motivated females to gain ICT skills, and participated in 47 team competitions. So this entire era turned out to be a blessing in disguise for me, as I was able to learn things that I couldn't previously. Here's something that I wrote about Covid-19 while also learning how to write poetry.

The Year 2020

became the year we lost.
The year we lost our freedom, family members
employment, education,
security and sanity.
But the year we lost our freedom,
we gained wings to creativity.
The year we lost our family members,
we gained closer relationships and bonds.
The year we lost employment,
we gained ideas to do the impossible
and never give up.
The year we lost education,
we gained its value.
The year we lost our security
and became insecure,
we gained support from people unknown.
The year we lost our sanity,
we gained sensitization towards our mother,
Mother Earth!
So we gained
VALUES
VIRTUES
GRATITUDE
RESPECT
LOVE

The Year We Lost Was Actually The Year We Gained

Art By- Namya Joshi

Moving Towards Entrepreneurship
Chapter 10

"Entrepreneurship is living a few years of your life like most people won't so that you can spend the rest of your life like most people can't."
Anonymous

Entrepreneurship is vital because it has the potential to raise living standards and generate money, not only for entrepreneurs but also for connected firms. Entrepreneurs also contribute to change through innovation, as new and improved products enable the creation of new markets. Entrepreneurs use organisational abilities like planning, organising, and controlling to fill in the holes in the market economy. Small firms must contribute to employment, innovation, competition, and social and political stability for entrepreneurship to contribute to the economy. Seeing the rise of entrepreneurship during the shutdown inspired me to learn more about the fundamentals of entrepreneurship. I had entered one of the competitions for India's Top 20 Under 20 Children. As a result, I learned about the Young CEO program, which was hosted by the competition's organizers. I applied for it and I learned a lot. If I put my learning in words;

- Be specific about your aspirations.
- Write it down on a piece of paper.
- Come up with compelling reasons why you must achieve your goals.
- Make a clear plan and implement it on a daily basis.
- Keep meticulous records of your development.
- Be a pro at time management.
- Make business canvas models.
- Use the 4C's (Critical Thinking, Creativity, Collaboration, Communication) whenever possible.

Finally,
Making Your Dreams A Reality

I also learned a lot about creative thinking, freedom, generational wealth, expansion, flexibility, control, numerous streams of income, excitement, Ikigai (my favourite book), dreaming, creating, growing, managing, and a lot of other cool stuff. Most importantly I learned what it requires to make a company. As a result, I created the #EachOneTeachTen Club, which sells my merchandise. That was shared with my Young CEO Program teacher, who was ecstatic to see it. All proceeds from this merchandise are donated to animal welfare organisations. My entire experience learning about entrepreneurship has been incredible.

Quote By- Unknown
Art By - Namya Joshi

Tweet By- Mr. Narendra Modi,
Prime Minister Of India

Satyan Namya Joshi Honoured with Global Child Prodigy Award 2022

Ludhiana : Satyan Namya Joshi of Grade X of Sat Paul Mittal School brought laurels to the school once more as she was honoured with Global Child Prodigy Award 2022 on 20th August, 2022. Namya has been awarded with the Global Child Prodigy Award 2022 for her outstanding contribution and achievements in the field of Technology. The Global Child Prodigy Awards 2022 organized a grand ceremony at Marriot Hotel in Jaddaf to honor the awardees. Namya Joshi was honoured by Nobel Laureate Sir Richard J Roberts, Dr K Abdul Ghani, renowned environmentalist and 'Green Man of India', and Dr Azad Moopen, founder, chairman and managing director of Aster DM Healthcare.

GCP Awards is the world's first and only child prodigy initiative that recognizes the top 100 international child prodigies from various verticals each year. It is the first platform of its kind with the objective of recognizing child prodigies in different categories including Arts, Music, Dance, Writing, Modelling, Acting, Science, and Sports. This initiative aims at providing the young talent the global exposure they deserve while giving them the right opportunities at the right time to ensure that they create a major impact on the society. Namya Joshi, one of the top 100 Global Child Prodigies visited Dubai, UAE, for the award ceremony and showcased her extraordinary talent. The awardees came from different countries like the USA, France, Russia, India, Georgia, Kenya, Brazil, Greece, Belgium, Romania, and many more.Ms. Bhupinder Gogia, Principal, Sat Paul Mittal School, expressed her delight on Namya's outstanding accomplishment and congratulated her for this remarkable achievement.

Global Child Prodigy Award 2022

Namya Joshi of Sat Paul Mittal School, Ludhiana wins the Prestigious Diana Award

 by Online News India 6/29/2021 01:29:00 pm

Namya Joshi at the virtual award ceremony

Ludhiana, June 29, 2021 (News Team) Namya Joshi, aged 14, of Sat Paul Mittal School, Ludhiana, Punjab has been honoured with the prestigious Diana Award for going above and beyond daily life to create and sustain positive change. The Diana Award is the highest accolade a young person can achieve for social action or humanitarian efforts. Established in memory of Diana, Princess of Wales, the Award is given out by the charity of the same name and has the support of both her sons, The Duke of Cambridge and The Duke of Sussex.

There were 12 Diana Award Judging Panels representing each UK region or nation and a further three panels representing countries outside of the UK. Each panel consist of three judges: one young person, an education or youth work professional, and a business or government representative. Nominations were judged using the Criteria Guide and Scoring Guide which had been created to measure quality of youth social action.

Tessy Ojo, CEO of The Diana Award, during the Virtual Award ceremony held on 28th June, 2021, congratulated the Diana Award recipients from the UK and around the globe who are changemakers for their generation. She said that by receiving the honour they would inspire more young people to get involved in their communities and begin their own journey as active citizens. For over twenty years, the Diana Award has valued and invested in young people encouraging them to continue to make positive change in their communities and lives of others.

Namya shared that technology could be used to benefit mankind, but it was not until she started playing the computer-based game Minecraft, she realized how tech could be a powerful tool for learning. Namya has now trained more than 1,000 teachers and students on how Game Based Learning can be used in education. Namya has been applauded for her 'entrepreneurial spirit' and her ability to 'step into other people's shoes' as with her motto #EachOneTeachTen she shares her message of gaming for good. Namya Joshi had also won Pradhan Mantri Rashtriya Bal Puraskar earlier this year.

Diana Award, 2021

Namya Joshi awarded with a Platinum Medal at Sat Paul Mittal School

Ludhiana : A Felicitation function was organized at Sat Paul Mittal School to acknowledge and applaud Satyan Namya Joshi for her exemplary achievements in the field of technology and innovation. She was awarded with a Platinum Medal for her noteworthy contribution and service to the cause of education in STEM. The award is an epitome of excellence given only to the highest deserving candidates who have made the school proud by their commendable achievements and contribution. The function was graced by Shri Rakesh Bharti Mittal, Chairman, Governing Council, Sat Paul Mittal School, Mr. Bipin Gupta, Vice Chairman and other members of the Governing Council, Members of the Academic Advisory Council, and Members of the Nehru Sidhant Kender Trust. The gala celebrations began with a dance performance invoking Lord Ganesh's blessing. This was followed by a welcome address by the worthy Chief Guest, Shri Rakesh Bharti Mittal. Shri Rakesh Bharti Mittal congratulated Namya on her achievements and her dedication to her vision to change the world with the potent weapon of education. A live podcast with Shri Rakesh Bharti Mittal, Chairman, Governing Council which was indeed insightful and refreshing. Ms Bhupinder Gogia, Principal, Sat Paul Mittal School proposed a vote of thanks and also congratulated Namya and her parents for bringing laurels to the school.

Platinum Award, Sat Paul Mittal School

Milestones
Chapter 11

As you work toward huge milestones, be grateful for all of the minor successes, since it's not the finale that matters most, but how you got there.
Namya Joshi

#EachOneTeachTen was inspired by my personal credo. I have mentored and trained over 10,000 teachers and students – 1510 girls, 3350 educators, and 4960 kids – in my region, country, and around the world to produce game-based lessons for use in classrooms. Every action we take has an impact on those around us. Is it true that you are conscious of your impact? I was awarded the Pradhan Mantri Rashtriya Bal Puraskar, India's highest civilian honour for an individual under the age of 18 years old, for my continued efforts to create and empower others.

On the 24th of January 2021, my mother received a message inviting her to join a WhatsApp group, and I'll never forget it. The message she received led my mother to inquire, "Who is this?" and if this was the final list. She went to her workplace after that and I had my online classes. I turned on my laptop to make my daily to-do list. My eyes were opened wide when I received an email from the Prime Minister's office informing me that I had been selected as one of 32 awardees from across India. I met our worthy Prime Minister Mr. Narender Modi and his words: "Punjab's Daughter-Namya Joshi" still echoes in my ears. The tweet from his personal account congratulating me as "Ludhiana's gamer Namya Joshi again proved there is no girl or boy gamer. A gamer is just a gamer."

Winning the Bal Puraskar Award has paved the way for me to continue advocating for STEM education, and as a result, on November 14th, 2020, I started the STEM podcast,

#EachOneTeachTen An Amazing World of Stem. This podcast reaffirmed my belief that STEM can be integrated into all classrooms and households, regardless of subject or grade level. How amazing that a student and a teacher are discussing and reaching out to educators and students all across the world through this podcast to spread the word that STEM can assist all educators in providing possibilities for their children to study and manage their own learning. Before I knew it, two years had passed and I'd completed 50 episodes of my podcast. The Diana Award and the Global Child Prodigy Award are validation of my efforts, and they encourage me to continue on my path.

My internship at Piispala Youth Summer Camp in Finland during my summer break will forever be unforgettable. The fifteen-day experience helped me to sharpen my skills and enhance my productivity. I was part of the Youth Work, Internationalism and Instruction Service Department wherein my role was to meet different people coming from different countries and collaborate with them to create Virtual Youth Centre Piispala in Minecraft. I was allocated a specific workplace to work at too! I trained the members of Piispala, POKE, and Leader Viisari to work in multiplayer and took coding workshops for them. In addition to getting to meet new people from around the world, this internship gave me the chance to improve my communication, time management, creative, and critical thinking abilities. It helped me understand how to meet the organisation's requirements. To maintain the work-life balance, I was involved in various excursions, adventures, sports, and activities like playing basketball everyday, canoeing and camping in the lake near the camp, throwing a frisbee in the forest, bowling, making objects into 3D models, making jewellery, archery, sup boarding, fishing, attending Finnish Summer Festival, t-shirt painting, rock climbing, engraving art, and lake swimming that took care of my well being.

Gratitude is the sweetest blossom that springs from the soul. I want to give back to society whatever I have received. I'm a social entrepreneur with my own line of merchandise. The proceeds from this merchandise are contributed to a non-profit organisation that cares for animals. I am a believer of the adage, "Stay true to yourself, yet always open to learn, work hard and never give up your dreams, even if nobody else believes." - Philip Sweet

Quote By- Unknown
Art By - Namya Joshi

#EachOneTeachTen

Final Thoughts

Let Opportunity Be Your Biscuit

Opportunities are windows of possibilities for something good to happen, but you must seize them!
Namya Joshi

Leaders value opportunities because the people they lead value them as well. Opportunities are places where people can try new things, improve their skills, and perhaps discover themselves. Thus it is important to grab opportunities since they knock very softly. "Grab the opportunity," says the narrator. Right, how many times have you heard that? But what exactly does it imply? Would you recognise one if you came across one? Life is the most incredible gift we've been given. Recognising that is the first step. Step two is to take advantage of all of God's incredible possibilities for growth. It is, however, our obligation to perceive them, seize them, and then act rationally on them. The majority of individuals either aren't paying attention or are unaware of the significance of opportunities. They respond to opportunities with a sluggishness that lasts for a long period. Simply expressed, "we shall accomplish enormous success in our lives if we seize the appropriate chance at the right moment." So, let your opportunity be your biscuit before the biscuit falls in the tea because then you would neither have the biscuit nor the tea.

Quote By- Unknown
Art By - Namya Joshi

Take Vitamins Not Painkillers

Time isn't the main thing. It's the only thing."
Miles Davis

Never heard this phrase before? Well, let me explain it to you. Here's a situation. You are given a task to be completed and submitted ten days later. Would you rather start working a little bit on that task from the day you received it or do it one day before submission? Well if you would do it one day before, you take Painkillers. But, if you start from the day assigned by giving a little time to it day by day, you love to take in Vitamins. That's exactly what the phrase means. Do not be a person who starts things at the deadline but the person who is already done with the work before the deadline. I used to take painkillers, but as time passed, I realized they weren't good for me or my personality, so I switched to vitamins, which helped me keep my routine effective.

Art By - Namya Joshi

ON & ON & ON...

I aspire to be an empowered woman with vision and grace. Soft-hearted, self-aware, and sure. Respected for my mind, admired for my heart and above all, always honest, open and raw.
Namya Joshi

My role models are girls who desire to be successful in life, those who have taken that sense of conviction and have broken the ceiling and have taken that extra step towards innovation in life. So I am grateful to all those girls who worked hard for their victory after all their failures and never gave up. Here, I discuss my experiences as an Indian and a Global Citizen. By living up to our Prime Minister Mr. Narendra Modi's vision of Atma Nirbhar Bharat and Digital India, I hope to propel my country forward in the realm of technology. The goal of Atma Nirbhar Bharat is to make the country and its people self-sufficient in every way. The goal of the Digital India initiative is to make India a digitally empowered society with a knowledge economy.

I also want to fulfill my responsibilities as a global citizen, which include the responsibility to understand one's own and others' perspectives; to protect the principle of cultural diversity; to make connections and build social and working relationships with people from other countries and cultures; to comprehend the ways in which people and countries around the world are interconnected and interdependent; to comprehend leading global issues and their national impact, and to understand the ways in which people and countries around the world are interconnected and interdependent. I want to develop a Universal Education System that anyone may access, regardless of caste, gender, creed, or ethnicity. It would be a platform where gamified lesson plans for all grade levels and all sorts of educational systems around the world would be available. I've already started working on it because the end is always positive when something is done with patience and effort; Take Vitamins, Not Painkillers. After all this, I want to give a house in the mountains to mom, so she can enjoy it with a cup of coffee in her hand while enjoying the sunrise for all her small little pampering and sacrifices. It we realize these sacrifices at the right time then life is much more divine.

#EachOneTeachTen
and The Journey Continues

Quote By- Mary Engelbriet
Art By- Namya Joshi

A Call To Action

Alert, Balanced, Engaged, Informed, Inclusive and An Impactor, that's a Leader. Each time a person stands up for an idea or acts to improve a lot of others, he sends forth a tiny ripple of hope and cross each other from a million different centers of energy and daring, those ripples build a current. You create positive ripples into this world every time you offer a kind word, loving action, an empowering insight or smile because whoever receives it passes it on to someone else, who then passes it on, who then passes it on, who then passes it on, who then passes it on. When we inspire youth to pursue careers in STEM we, Break Through the Ceiling. I was inspired by an incident. Who knows the next person out of you might be inspired by another....have faith and belief and see the magic happening in your life. Thousands of candles can be lit from a single candle and the life of the candle will never be shortened. I believe in Share Learn and Grow. So let's EachOneTeachTen and empower others.

I ENCOURAGE YOU TO FOLLOW YOUR PASSIONS AND SHARE THOSE PASSIONS WITH OTHERS. SHARE YOUR LEARNING JOURNEY WITH OTHERS AS WE CONTINUE TO BUILD THE #EACHONETEACHTEN MOVEMENT.

Community Connect - Humanizing The Effect Of #EachOneTeachTen

EICHER SCHOOL
(Affiliated with C.B.S.E.)
NO. CBSE AFF/96/630056/2041-44
Parwanoo, Distt. Solan (H.P.) - 173 220
Ph.: +91-94594-93393
E-mail : eicherschool@gmail.com
eicherschoolpwn@rediffmail.com

Ref.No. ESP/06/2021/.   Dated 03/06/2021

Appreciation Certificate

This is to certify that Miss Namya Joshi conducted a webinar on "Learning the nuances of podcast" on June 1st 2021 for all the teachers of Eicher School Parwanoo.

I congratulate Namya for facilitating the learning of Podcasting in a very engaging and sequential manner

In this webinar teachers could understand: how to record a podcast, how to find a suitable hosting site and basic understanding of editing the podcast. Teachers also got exposed to a host of apps and resources for creating a good podcast.

On behalf of the entire staff of Eicher School Parwanoo, I wish Namya all the best wishes for her future endeavours.

(Deepak Singl)
Principal

Having Namya in our Future technologies class and workshops has been always a big boost. A child who always kept us at Digilab work harder to adept with the game based learning. I have seen Namya grow phenomenally in the past years wherein she has worked selflessly for not only the students but also for teachers across the globe. Having her as a mentor for Minecraft, has made us more professional and we have used her maps as examples. More important is that we empower our students and teachers what young people can do.

I have seen Namya grow into a force to reckon with in the field of empowering others through her resilience and passion of spreading the message of #EachOneTeachTen. Namya has soared high in the field by being a speaker at various national and international events and inspired a lot of students and helped them to excel in the STEM field. Her collaborations with other professionals have paved a way for others to follow on her footsteps. What Namya has achieved should be emulated and I am sure that Namya is so passionate and humble that she would herself help other people to achieve this. This will happen soon at our international Future work project. I am happy that I would always be called Namya's teacher but I am even more proud that I can call Namya my teacher.

Pekka Ouli
pekka.ouli@poke.fi

Er. Surinder Singh Virdi
FIE
B.Sc Engg (Civil) M.Sc Engg (Hydraulics & Irrig.)
D.H.E. Delft (Hydrology) Holland
Specialised in Land Drainage, Holland

199. Sector 16-A, CHANDIGARH - 160015
Res: 0172-2780744
Off 0172-2702553, 2715073
Fax 0172-2702553 Mob. 9417304482
E-mail agolho22@gmail.com

Dear Namya Joshi,

Read in the newspapers regarding Mr. Satya Nadella, CEO Microsoft talking about your project and appreciating how you are in a position to enjoy Minecraft and then effectively learn programming.

It is a very great honour for you, your family & school in which you are studying.

We pray to God Almighty to bless you to achieve greater heights in name & fame by learning Minecraft its programming.

with lots of love & regards

Yours Sincerely,

(Er. Surinder Singh Virdi)
Former Senator & Syndic,
Punjab University

Namya Joshi,
Student 7th Grade.
Sat Paul Mittal School,
Phase 2, Urban Estate,
Dugri, Ludhiana(Pb.)

#EachOneTeachTen Anthem

Global goals for noble souls,
Transforming our world,
to a better wonder to behold.

No poverty, zero hunger,
for people all ages,
the elderly or younger.

Good health and well-being,
some quality education.
That is worth seeing!

To empower women and girls,
snd ensure they be free-spirited and swirl.

Clean water and sanitation,
ss it not the right of every nation?

Economic growth, inclusive and sustained,
through industry, innovation and infrastructure be gained!

Reduce inequality for sure,
make cities and human settlements safe and secure!

Take urgent actions to combat climate change,
conserve life below water and land, ensure we do not estrange!

Justice for all, oh Peaceful and empathetic nations. Let us all
partner to achieve these goals, And provide much needed
SALVATION!

About the Author
Namya Joshi

Namya is a Grade X student at Sat Paul Mittal School, India. In 2023, she is 16 years old and the official Minecraft Student Ambassador by Microsoft. Inspired by her own motto #EachOneTeachTen, She has spent the last five years designing and delivering free-of-cost coding workshops for more than 15,000 teachers and young people, especially girls, in India and all over the world, as well as empowering other young people to run their own coding clubs. She has raised awareness about social issues using game-based learning with STEM to solve humanity's problems.

She has been honoured with the prestigious Pradhanmantri Rashtriya Bal Puraskar 2021, Diana Award 2021, Global Child Prodigy Award 2022, and Global Impactor Student IMPACT Award 2021. She is honored to be the UNESCO World Youth Multimedia Competition winner, TeachSDGs Ambassador, Rex Karamaveer Bronze Medal Awardee, Global E-Innovation Award Winner, and Youngest Global Juror. She is the first ever student to attain the Adobe Creative Educator certifications – ACE1 and ACE 2.

She is proud to serve in numerous reputable organizations as a board member, advisory member, and member. She is a dynamic speaker and has presented about the potential of STEM and game-based learning at events such as KEOS2019 Finland, EduDays Microsoft, UNESCO, ISTE, CSLA, CONVOKE, Asia Berlin

Summit, EdChatInteractive, Azure Conference, Global Maker Day, Digital Citizen Summit and Adobe Education Summit.

Her Hobbies

She is an orator, dramatist, dancer, writes poetry, sketch artist, yoga player, skater, swimmer, badminton, passionate basketball player, and a voracious reader.

Her favorite quote

Stay true to yourself, yet always open to learning, Work hard and never give up your dreams, even if nobody else believes

Website	YouTube Channel	Podcast	Minecraft Lessons	Merch

About the Editor

Sarah Laliberte has worked as a writer and editor in the publishing industry for over 18 years. She brings a passion for words to her writing and editing in order to create clear and engaging content. Sarah enjoys helping other writers bring their writing into focus, and she aims to share information and ideas in a way that tickles readers' brains. Sarah is an alumni of the North Carolina School of Science and Mathematics and the University of North Carolina at Chapel Hill. She currently lives in the Blue Ridge Mountains of North Carolina.

View our services, catalog of books, and
meet our team of authors at
https://xfactoredu.org.

Our team of educators are using their
voice, journey, experiences, and
practices to be the catalyst for change
in education.

Visit: https://xfactoredu.org

More from X-Factor Publishing

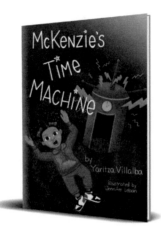

CODE BREAKER LEADERSHIP SERIES

CODE BREAKER KID COLLECTION

CODE BREAKER INC.

Breaking code isn't just about programming, it's about disrupting the status quo. It is about challenging social norms. It is about having critical conversations. It is about challenging systematic beliefs. It is about educating the whole child - mind, body, and soul.

To learn more about
CODE BREAKER INC.
and our services,
visit www.codebreakeredu.com

INSPIRE · INNOVATE

LEAD · TEACH · LEARN

Made in the USA
Middletown, DE
13 January 2023

22113289R00051